Lessons From Life

52 Short Devotionals

By Don Lawrence

Introduction

We read in the Gospels that Jesus told many, many parables. Parables have been described as earthly stories with a heavenly meaning. As Jesus traveled, he'd see an everyday occurrence, from which, he would teach a lesson to His disciples. A farmer planting seeds, birds feeding on grain, fishermen casting a net, a poor widow giving an offering at the temple, lilies growing in a field, a fig tree with no fruit, guests selecting the honored seats at a table, dirty feet unwashed by a host, a shepherd looking for a lost sheep, a mustard seed, a vineyard, a lost coin, a small child... the list goes on and on. Lessons to be learned from everyday occurrences - I call them, "Lessons From Life." Jesus used the things of life to teach spiritual lessons.

I believe these lessons are all around us. We are in the midst of them every day. They are where we live, where we work, where we travel. They are opportunities to challenge us, encourage us, warn us, educate and enlighten us. They are lessons from life.

In this book I have compiled fifty-two such lessons. Lessons I have experienced in my own life. They are intended to be a quick, two to three minute read, fifty-two short devotionals. I hope that you will enjoy reading them as much as I enjoyed experiencing them and writing about them.

A fellow traveler in life,
Don Lawrence

Parasailing

Now I know how a kite feels! One of the highlights on a recent trip to the Florida Keys was a fun adventure of parasailing. Neither my wife Lisa nor I had ever been parasailing and we were excited to give it a try. We boarded our boat with our two guides and two other adventurers. We left the harbor in Key West and headed out to open water. The two ladies who were on the boat with us were the first to go up on the tandem parasail ride. Then it was our turn.

Our guides strapped us in and gave us our final instructions. The boat turned into the wind and then the massive sail billowed behind us. Slowly the crank let out the rope and we were airborne.

The captain of the boat would speed up or slow down, causing us to rise or descend. At one point he went slow enough to allow us to skim across the surface of the water. It was as if we were walking on waves. Then he would accelerate and we would climb high into the sky. What a view!

Little gusts of wind would buffet us just a bit, right or left, up or down. I remember thinking, "This must be how a kite feels, bouncing around in the wind." I was glad we were securely strapped in and tied to the boat with a very strong rope. Otherwise, a strong gust of wind could have been disastrous.

The Apostle Paul warns us of another type of wind and waves when he writes, "Then we will no longer be infants, tossed back and forth by the waves, and blown here and there by every wind of teaching and by the cunning and craftiness of men in their deceitful scheming." Ephesians 4:14.

The Apostle Paul explains that the mature Christian isn't deceived by every deceitful doctrine which blows across our path. We are to be securely grounded in Biblical truth concerning the essentials of our Christian faith. Make no mistake about it, false doctrines are constantly blowing about, testing and buffeting those of faith. It is critical to be well grounded in Biblical truth. The good news is that the

1

more securely grounded one is, the higher and more exhilarating their spiritual flight can be.

Get your doctrine securely strapped into Biblical truth, then hang on for an incredible adventure and enjoy the view!

Kayaking

Approximately one and a half hours north of our home here in Arizona, Lisa and I were kayaking on the Verde River near a town called Cottonwood. The area was beautiful and the weather was fantastic; we had a great time. The river was very calm with a couple of mild rapids.   We were on the water for about an hour and very much enjoyed the experience.

Of course, kayaking includes paddling. We could have just allowed the current to carry us downstream, but that can lead to trouble. There were a couple of whirlpools to avoid, some overhanging branches to steer clear of, several protruding rocks that we needed to go around, etc. Even in the rapids there are certain sides which are preferable. Paddling doesn't merely move the kayak, it gives direction. It ensures that we get where we want to go.

Too many people in life simply, "go with the flow." They allow the currents of life to dictate where they are going in life. They have no direction, no purpose, no goals. They have no idea where they will end up because they have no idea what they want to do with their life. As such, it is not surprising that so many end up in trouble. While overhanging branches, whirlpools, and protruding rocks are three dangers on a river, life is filled with hundreds of dangers for the life lived without purpose or direction.

So, what is your purpose in life? In what direction are you heading? What are your goals? How will you steer clear of potential problems? How will you traverse the rapids when they come your way?

The Psalmist prayed to God, "I pray to you, O Lord, in the time of your favor; in your great love, O God, answer me with your sure salvation. Rescue me from the mire, do not let me sink; deliver me from those who hate me, from the deep waters. Do not let the flood waters engulf me or the depths swallow me up or the pit close its mouth over me." Psalm 69:13-15.

Life is filled with challenges which can easily consume one

without direction. Where do you hope to be at the end of your life's journey?

Jesus said, "Do not let your hearts be troubled. Trust in God; trust also in me. In my Father's house are many rooms; if it were not so, I would have told you. I am going there to prepare a place for you. And if I go and prepare a place for you, I will come back and take you to be with me that you also may be where I am." John 14:1-3.

Not only will Jesus guide you through (not always around, but oftentimes through) the troubles of life, but He also gives the ultimate direction in life. A home in heaven awaits for those who know Jesus as their Lord and Savior! Paddle in that direction and you'll traverse the challenges in the river of life.

Olympic Athletes

On a, "watch-the-leaves-change-colors" trip, Lisa and I spent a few days at Lake Placid, New York. Lake Placid hosted two Winter Olympics: 1932 and 1980. I really enjoy watching the bobsled races during the Olympics, and thus was thrilled that we had the opportunity to ride the Olympic bobsled there. (It was on wheels, but it was the same type of sled on the exact track on which the Olympic competitions were held. What a thrill!)   I also enjoy watching Olympic Ice Hockey. To visit the site of the "Miracle on Ice," was another highlight of our visit. Other events I enjoy watching are speed skating, down hill skiing, snow boarding, and of course, the Jamaican bobsled team. Ya-mon! Lisa likes figure skating, which I don't care too much for. But then, I enjoy curling, which she finds boring. (Notice they never show slow-motion replays in curling? The whole thing is slow-motion!)

Regardless of the sport, these athletes are the very best in the world. They have several things in common. You can talk about their passion, the sacrifice they make, the hard work involved to get to that level, the support of their family, the ability to overcome setbacks and injuries and disappointments, and many other things. Included in that list is the critical component we call self-discipline.

It takes a tremendous amount of self-discipline to put in the thousands of hours of practice, training, conditioning, working out, and studying. It also takes self-discipline to stick to their diets, to eat healthy meals, to avoid junk food. It takes self-discipline to be able to devote as much time to their sport as they do and still handle all the other responsibilities in their life: education, jobs and family. Self-discipline is essential to be a successful Olympic athlete.

In fact, I'd say that self-discipline is essential to be successful in any area of your life, such as: education, career, relationships, finance, health, etc. It is certainly critical in your spiritual life.

Discipline is a critical part of daily prayer and Bible study, participation in weekly worship, participation in group Bible studies, serving in any area of ministry, financial stewardship and witnessing. If you want to be a winner, if you want to be successful, if you want the victory, self-discipline is one of the essentials!

The Apostle Paul wrote, "Do you not know that in a race all the runners run, but only one gets the prize? Run in such a way as to get the prize. Everyone who competes in the games goes into strict training. They do it to get a crown that will not last; but we do it to get a crown that will last forever."   1 Corinthians 9:24-25.

Animal Experiences

When he was three years old, Lisa and I took our grandson, Caleb, to the zoo. We enjoyed watching him see the elephants, lions, zebras, monkeys, giraffes, various reptiles, assorted birds, and many other animals. He especially liked the farm animals at the petting zoo. Touching the sheep, goats, cows, and horses was a special treat.

The following Sunday, after church, we took Caleb to the Rain Forest Café for lunch. Interspersed among their forest decor are man-made animals which move by man-made electronics and hydraulics and make sounds through man-made audio systems. It was interesting to watch Caleb as he was fascinated by the animals, not sure if they were real or not.

In both instances Caleb was very entertained and seemed to have a great time. One day he saw real, live animals. The other day he saw man-made animals.

This got me to thinking: The way people experience God is very similar to Caleb's animal experience. Some experience the real, true, living God. Others settle for a man-made God and a man-made experience. Simply stated, that is the difference between Christianity and the various religions of the world.

Christianity is, of course, all about Jesus Christ, the fullness of Deity in bodily form. He could be seen, heard, touched, and interacted with. No intelligent person denies the historical reality of Jesus Christ. Thousands saw him. Many wrote about Him. He can withstand the scrutiny of investigation. Conversely, religions are typically built upon the strange experience of one individual, void of any other witnesses. The gullible, the deceived, line up to experience these man-made religious experiences. But that's as far as it goes. Their's is not eternal, it is not real, it is not permanent.

Christianity provides a vibrant relationship with the living God. The Apostle John writes, "That which was from the beginning, which we have heard, which we have seen with our eyes, which we have looked at and our hands have touched — this we proclaim concerning the Word of life. The life appeared; we have seen it and testify to it, and we proclaim to you the eternal life, which was with the Father and has appeared to us. We proclaim to you what we have seen and heard, so that you also may have fellowship with us. And our fellowship is with the Father and with his Son, Jesus Christ." 1 John 1:1-3

The Rain Forest Café imitates real animals. Entertaining, yes, but real, not at all. Religions are merely imitations of the real thing. Entertaining for some, but void of a real God experience. Jesus said, "...Anyone who has seen Me, has seen the Father..." And "I and the Father are One." John 14:9 and John 10:30.

If you want to worship the one true God, if you want to pray to the real God, if you want to live in heaven eternally with the one authentic God, Jesus Christ is the key.

He's the real deal - Jesus Christ is Lord!

The Sea of Cortez

Lisa and I have been visiting Rocky Point, Mexico for over twenty-five years. Rocky Point, or Puerto Penasco, is located on the northern end of the Sea of Cortez, also known as the Gulf of California. On our visits, one of the things we enjoy are sightings of dolphins and an occasional sea lion swimming by. It wasn't that long ago that one would rarely, if ever, see these wonderful creatures. We are told that lax environmental restrictions and lax enforcement of environmental law caused too much pollution to be dumped into the Sea of Cortez. The smaller marine life was devastated, which slowly impacted the entire food chain. Dolphins, sea lions, and even whales in the area became very scarce.

To the credit of the governing authorities, stricter laws were eventually passed and enforced and over time the waters became cleaner and more inhabitable for marine life of all shapes and sizes. Plant life and smaller fish began to flourish, which eventually led to the return of larger animals. All because the decision was made to clean up that which was being poured into the environment.

The same holds true for your own life. Various pollutants allowed into your life have far reaching consequences. Conversely, cleaning up what you allow to enter your life will have wonderful, positive effects. It is reversible! These pollutants include a variety of things, such as, books and magazines you read, music you listen to, movies and television shows you watch. Also, people you allow to influence you can be a source of "pollutants" in your life. (Don't be misled; peer pressure impacts adults as much as teenagers.) Your own thoughts and attitudes, if not cleansed, can have their own negative impact.

The quality of your life is precious. Guard it, protect it, and defend it. You deserve the abundant life Jesus Christ wants to earnestly give you (John 10:10). The Apostle Paul wrote,"Do not conform any longer to the pattern of this world, but be transformed by the renewing of your mind..." Romans 12:2.

Over time, the entire Sea of Cortez has been renewed. Dolphins are again plentiful. Sea lions have returned. Whales make their migratory visits. An abundance of small fish feed the large flocks of pelicans.

Your mind, in fact, your life, can experience a complete regeneration. The Bible states, "Therefore, if anyone is in Christ, he is a new creation; the old has gone, the new has come!" 2 Corinthians 5:17.

You can experience revitalization, renewal, and restoration. Remove the pollutants. Saturate your life with healthy influences. Then, enjoy life as God intended!

Beautiful Roses

My wife loves her roses! She has about forty rose bushes around our house. Yep, I actually counted them! A typical Saturday morning will find her working in her rose gardens: cutting, pruning, trimming, spraying, and whatever else they may need. Her roses oftentimes end up in vases in our home. They are beautiful!

One Saturday she asked me if the front drip system was working properly. I assured her that it was. She stated that the flower beds and the rose bushes seemed a little dryer than they should and asked if I'd check the system. I assured her that it was working and suggested that high temperatures were the reason for the dryness. She smiled and asked if I'd please check to make sure it was working properly.

So I did. Sure enough, the pressure regulator for the drip system had a huge crack in it and water was gushing out from it. Thus, no water was getting to the planter boxes. Lisa could tell that the roses were lacking water simply by looking at them. Without water, they begin to wither and eventually will die.

Within every human being is a soul which thirsts for spiritual water, a thirst which can only be quenched by God, Himself. The Psalmist stated, "As the deer pants for streams of water, so my soul pants for you, O God.   My soul thirsts for God, for the living God. When can I go and meet with God?" Psalm 42:1-2. We read in the Gospel of John, "On the last and greatest day of the Feast, Jesus stood and said in a loud voice, 'If anyone is thirsty, let him come to me and drink. Whoever believes in me, as the Scripture has said, streams of living water will flow from within him.'"   John 7:37-38.

If the thirst of the soul for spiritual water is not met, that soul will eventually wither and die. But spiritual water can be found in abundance, providing sustenance that not only quenches, but does so eternally.

Jesus said, "Whoever drinks the water I give him will never

thirst. Indeed, the water I give him will become in him a spring of water welling up to eternal life." John 4:14.

The source of eternal, living, soul satisfying water is Jesus Christ our Lord. The Apostle Paul wrote, "...They drank from the spiritual rock that accompanied them, and that rock was Christ." 1 Corinthians 10:4.

Do the flowers of your soul seem to be a bit dried and withered? Perhaps it's time to check their source of water!

My Grandson

One of the fun things about having a grandson is that I get to be like a kid again. Playing with toy cars and trucks, running through the sprinkler, watching cartoons, building forts, playing hide and seek, snacking on Animal Crackers, ... Kids have so many cool toys these days. I'm loving it!

My grandson doesn't need to worry about where his next meal is coming from. He doesn't need to worry about having enough clothes to wear. When he takes a leap of faith from the couch into my arms, he knows I will catch him. I guarantee it!

One of the cool things about becoming a Christian is that you get to be like a kid again. Jesus made an interesting observation about children. "Jesus called a little child and had him stand among them. And he said: 'I tell you the truth, unless you change and become like little children, you will never enter the kingdom of heaven. Therefore, whoever humbles himself like this child is the greatest in the kingdom of heaven." Matthew 18:2-4.

One aspect of our relationship with Jesus is that we can act like kids again. We don't need to worry about tomorrow. Jesus said, "Therefore do not worry about tomorrow, for tomorrow will worry about itself." Matthew 6:34.

We don't need to worry about our food or clothing. Jesus will provide a way for us to acquire what we need. Jesus said, "Therefore I tell you, do not worry about your life, what you will eat or drink; or about your body, what you will wear. Is not life more important than food, and the body more important than clothes? Look at the birds of the air; they do not sow or reap or store away in barns, and yet your heavenly Father feeds them. Are you not much more valuable than they?" Matthew 6:25-26.

And when we take a leap of faith into eternity, Jesus is there to catch us. He guarantees it! "Jesus said to her, 'I am the resurrection and the life. He who believes in me will live, even though he dies; and whoever lives and believes in me will never die..."'" John 11:25-26.

Whether it's playing with my grandson or running with Jesus, I'm loving being a kid again.

Childlike faith? I'm all for it! How about you?

Dennis's Boat

Recently I spent a weekend fishing at Lee's Ferry in northern Arizona with my son-in-law Josh and my friend Dennis. We left very early in the morning and arrived with enough time to get in a good half day of fishing. We picked up Dennis's boat from the storage lot and went to the boat ramp and launched it. Soon, we were in the boat idling away from the dock, getting ready to head upstream.

But then the motor stopped. Yes, it had gas. Yes, the two-cycle motor had oil in the reserve. It appeared that the motor had seized. It simply wouldn't run. Fortunately, there was an electric trolling motor which we used to get back to the dock. We put the boat back on the trailer and returned it to the storage lot.

We ended up renting a boat for the weekend and caught lots of fish. There was no one in the area who works on boats so we trailered it back home and Dennis took it into the shop to get it repaired. It turns out that a friend of Dennis's had used the boat and had run aground, breaking the propellor and bending the drive shaft. His friend replaced the propellor but did no further repairs. The motor ran, the propellor turned, so he thought everything was O.K.   He was wrong. As a result of the bent drive shaft, the engine seized and a major repair was required.

This reminds me of a lot of broken relationships. Sometimes people do "cosmetic" repairs but don't deal with the major issues lying just below the surface. "I'll smile and be pleasant," they reason, and thus they give the appearance of a "fixed" relationship. But things that are broken need to be repaired. Otherwise, the real problem continues to fester and it is just a matter of time before deeper issues become manifest. Honesty, clarifications, truth, apologies, forgiving, and reconciliation are all part of the repair process. But once repaired, the relationship can indeed run smoothly again.

The Apostle Peter wrote, "Finally, all of you, live in harmony with one another; be sympathetic, love as brothers, be compassionate and humble." 1 Peter 3:8.

Lord willing, we'll head back up to Lee's Ferry in the fall for some more fishing. This time with an engine that works well because it has been properly repaired.

Is there a relationship that needs repairing in your life?   It's worth the effort and energy to get it repaired correctly. Who knows, there may be a fishing trip in your future!

What A View!

We were 103 stories up, 1,353 feet high, looking straight down at the sidewalk and street below! I and my Associate Pastors, Gary, Chad and Randy, were in Chicago at the Willis Tower (formerly the Sears Tower). On the 103rd floor, they have large plexiglass boxes that extend about four feet out of the building, which one can walk into. The four of us waited in line and then stepped into the box.

Although we were very confident in the safety of those boxes, there was still a queasy feeling as you take that first step away from the safety of the building. Of course, we took pictures, and had our picture taken. It's not every day one can look literally straight down from such heights. It was pretty awesome.

It got me to wondering about what the view will be like during the rapture. The Apostle Paul wrote, "For the Lord himself will come down from heaven, with a loud command, with the voice of the archangel and with the trumpet call of God, and the dead in Christ will rise first. After that, we who are still alive and are left will be caught up together with them in the clouds to meet the Lord in the air. And so we will be with the Lord forever." 1 Thessalonians 4:16-17.

As we are "caught up," as we are headed toward the clouds, I imagine we'll be so enthralled with the returning Jesus that we'll be looking up, not down. But still, if we were to look down, what would we see? Will we have a queasy feeling, a feeling of sympathy, a feeling of compassion, for those left behind? Will we see a world in utter chaos? Will we in an instant realize how ridiculous some of our priorities, attitudes and interests were before that moment?

I suppose the more important question isn't speculation about what we will do then, but rather what are we doing now. Jesus said, "So you also must be ready, because the Son of Man will come at an hour when you do not expect him." Matthew 24:44.

Are you ready? Are there some things you need to change immediately? Are there some people you need to share Christ with, before it's too late? One of the last things recorded in the Bible are these words from our Lord, "He who testifies to these things says, 'Yes, I am coming soon.' Amen. Come, Lord Jesus!"   Revelation 22:20.

When Christ returns I hope to see many, many family and friends all around me, rising to meet the Lord in the air. We won't need a plexiglass box, airplane, hot air balloon, or wings. Our queasy feelings will be replaced with feelings of exhilaration. We'll rise to eternal life via the power and presence of Jesus. That's a view, and an experience, like no other!

Painting The House

Our old house was once again in need of a fresh coat of paint. As you know, there's more to painting a house than painting! The process begins with the selecting and hiring of a painter. Then, there is a great deal of prep work before the paint can be applied. We had to do a lot of trimming of flowers, bushes and trees to allow access to all of the walls. Then came the power washing, scraping, brushing, caulking, and minor repairs. And of course there is all of the masking and taping. Before any of that, we had to make our color selection and visit our local Property Association to obtain the proper permits. Eventually the paint was applied. They painted the entire house and trim, flower boxes, fences around the yard, wrought iron fence around the pool and the balcony... lots of paint!

But the project was not yet finished. It was now time for the cleanup and the returning of all of the items which had to be moved at the start of the project. Eventually, the project was completed. Our once Navajo White color has been covered with a rich Mocha Brown. The house looks beautiful.

This got me to thinking about a far more important color transformation that all Christians experience. We read in the book of Isaiah, "Though your sins are like scarlet, they shall be as white as snow; though they are red as crimson, they shall be like wool." Isaiah 1:18.

We are all colored by our sins: blood red. The problem is, our sinfulness precludes us from going to heaven. And, it can't be merely painted over. It (we) must be cleansed. The Apostle Paul writes, "...You were washed, you were sanctified, you were justified in the name of the Lord Jesus Christ and by the Spirit of our God." 1 Corinthians 6:11.

Unlike painting a house, there isn't a lot of work for us to do to secure this new spiritual "color." In fact, there is no work for us at all! "For it is by grace you have been saved, through faith — and this not from yourselves, it is the gift of God — not by works, so that no one

19

can boast." Ephesians 2:8-9.

We are "washed white as snow" by the work of Jesus Christ on the cross. "In him we have redemption through his blood, the forgiveness of sins, in accordance with the riches of God's grace that he lavished on us with all wisdom and understanding." Ephesians 1:7-8.

No amount of work, no amount of painting can cleanse us of our sins. But Jesus can. And He does. In His eyes, we look beautiful! What's the spiritual color of your soul? Is it time for a cleansing?

Earth To Mars

NASA landed a space craft called Curiosity on the surface of Mars late on a Sunday evening, August 5, 2012. A longtime friend as well as long time church member, Carl Nuckolls, worked on the communication system for Curiosity. Carl was a Senior Communications Engineer at General Dynamics at the time. I am fascinated by Carl's work and greatly impressed with his intelligence. (Especially in light of the fact I still struggle to understand some of the functions on my cell phone!)

Carl explained to me that it takes approximately seven minutes for the radio signal to reach from earth to Curiosity as it sits on Mars. Those radio waves travel at the speed of light. Compare that to the fact that it took Curiosity approximately eight months, traveling 352 million miles, to get to Mars. The radio signals are transmitted and received through a 70-meter-wide communications dish powered by several kilowatts of power. The whole Earth to Mars communication thing truly is incredible.

Another incredible form of communication is prayer. Think about it, a mere human being is able to communicate with the Creator of the universe! The Psalmist stated, "The righteous cry out, and the Lord hears them; he delivers them from all their troubles." Psalm 34:17.

In the New Testament, the Apostle John wrote, "This is the confidence we have in approaching God: that if we ask anything according to His will, He hears us." 1 John 5:14. Notice that word "confidence." It's a sure thing! Not because of our ability or our intelligence or our goodness. It's a sure thing because of who God is. It's a sure thing because of the indwelling presence of God's Holy Spirit. It's a sure thing because of God's incredible love, compassion and concern for every single human being that has ever been created. God hears your prayers!

Fortunately, for most of us, you don't have to be a rocket scientist nor a senior communications engineer to communicate with the Lord. You also don't need to be a pastor, a priest, or any other type of clergy. All you have to do is simply talk to God, and He hears you. Now THAT'S incredible!

Bubba

A guy named Bubba Watson won the 2012 PGA Masters Golf Tournament. I'm not making this up. Although it's not his legal name, he does go by Bubba. And he's a golfer. But I digress.

Bubba won the tournament on the second hole of the tie-breaker playoff. After his drive went into the woods, I thought for sure that he had lost the tournament. But then he hit an absolutely incredible shot that he had to curve around the trees, up the fairway, and onto the green. It truly was an amazing shot. After two putts, he was the champion. In just a matter of minutes he went from what most would call a hopeless situation to celebrating an incredible victory.

Oftentimes in life we get into a situation that many, if not most, might consider to be a hopeless predicament. But just like Bubba, we must never, ever give up. Never lose hope! Always keep trying. If we will do so, rewards will follow.

Have you ever been there? Are you there now? Lost in the woods, back to the wall, can't see your way out? Perhaps you can relate to the Apostle Paul when he wrote, "We are hard pressed on every side, but not crushed; perplexed, but not in despair; persecuted, but not abandoned; struck down, but not destroyed." 2 Corinthians 4:8-9.

Perhaps, like Paul, and Bubba, it might help to change your focus. Rather than being consumed by all the doom and gloom, it's time to start planning a way out, a way up, a way to victory. And then, put that plan into action.

Just a few verses later Paul wrote, "We live by faith, not by sight." 2 Corinthians 5:7.

Joshua faced a monumental challenge as the nation of Israel entered the promised land. The Lord encourage him, "Have I not commanded you? Be strong and courageous. Do not be terrified; do not be discouraged, for the Lord your God will be with you wherever you go." Joshua 1:9. In fact, three times in that first chapter of Joshua, the Lord says, "Be strong and courageous!"

God is greater than your challenges. He is greater than your problems. He is greater than your predicament. He is greater than your situation. He is greater than your set-back.

No matter where you are, don't lose heart. The Lord is with you! With Him on your side, victory is always possible!

The Great Chicago Fire

Lisa and I were in Chicago some time ago and while at their history museum I had the opportunity to read some of the details of the great Chicago fire of 1871. Sadly, the fire burned for three days destroying over 17,000 homes and buildings, killing over 300 individuals and leaving approximately 100,000 people homeless.

Like many of you, I had heard the story that the fire was started when Mrs. Catherine O'Leary's cow kicked over a lantern in her barn. I was surprised to find out that this simply isn't true. The reporter who originally wrote that story admitted some twenty years later that he made it all up. Approximately 126 years after the fire, in 1997 the Chicago City Council passed a resolution exonerating Mrs. O'Leary AND her cow!

How, then, did the fire start? No one is certain, but theories abound! Some have speculated that it was started by a wayward cigarette or the spark from a fireplace. One theory is that a thief stealing milk from the O'Leary barn knocked over a lantern that started the fire. Others have said that two men got in a fight over a game of cards and during their fight the lantern was knocked over. One individual has even proposed that a small meteor started the blaze!

Various theories notwithstanding, Mrs. O'Leary bore the blame, and subsequent wrath, of most of her community. Sadly, Mrs. O'Leary lived the rest of her life being blamed for an incredible tragedy that was not her fault.

The spreading of lies, rumors, and gossip can be very destructive. In fact, James uses the illustration of a fire when discussing this problem. "Likewise the tongue is a small part of the body, but it makes great boasts. Consider what a great forest is set on fire by a small spark. The tongue also is a fire, a world of evil among the parts of the body. It corrupts the whole person, sets the whole course of his life on fire, and is itself set on fire by hell." James 3:5-6.

You can help stop the fiery spread of rumors, gossip and

misinformation simply by not repeating every bit of juicy gossip or by not forwarding every politically motivated email that comes your way. Christians lose their integrity and credibility when they spread information that is not grounded in truth. This is not to say that we shouldn't engage, or even debate, current issues of our culture. But we must guard against repeating information that is urban legend or out and out misinformation. There is far too much at stake, too many people can get burned, and it can take many, many years to rebuild our credibility.

Simply stated, let's check our facts before fanning the flames.

My Bicycle

I recently purchased a slightly used Bianchi Imola. It's an Italian bicycle. I can't believe how light it is. It has three sprockets by the pedals and nine sprockets on the back wheel making it a 27 speed bike. The tires are super thin and hold 110 pounds per square inch of air pressure. This bike was made to be ridden and is built to go fast!

However, as sleek as this bicycle is, one fact about bicycles has not changed: the rider still must provide the pedal power. That would be me. The bike will only go as fast and as far as my old legs can crank the pedals around and around. My bike can help improve the condition of my heart, my legs, my lungs, and improve my endurance, but only if I ride it regularly.

This reminds me of your Bible. Some of you have a very slick looking Bible. It has study notes and maps and cross-reference keys. It might even have special tabs to help you find books in the Bible. Perhaps it even has a very beautiful leather cover. However, one fact about Bibles has not changed: The Bible doesn't do the owner any good unless the owner reads it. That would be you.

The Bible will only take you as far in your spiritual walk as you are willing to spend time reading and studying it. It can strengthen your spiritual maturity, it can help you resist temptations, it can help you to more consistently exude the fruits of the Spirit, and it can give you guidance and direction in life, but only if you read it regularly.

The Apostle Paul wrote to the church in Rome, "Everything that was written in the past was written to teach us, so that through endurance and the encouragement of the Scriptures we might have hope." Romans 15:4.

My bike is a beautiful blue color and is nice to look at. But bikes aren't meant to be looked at. They are meant to be ridden. Your Bible sitting on your coffee table might be nice to look at. However, Bibles aren't meant to be coffee table decorations. They are meant to be read.

As the Apostle Paul explained, "Consequently, faith comes from hearing the message, and the message is heard through the word of Christ." Romans 10:17.

Let me encourage you to take a spiritual spin in your Bible every morning. It's worth the ride!

Beautiful Music

A piano can make some very beautiful music. So can a saxophone. When played as a duet they produce something extra special. One Sunday morning at our church worship service, we enjoyed such a treat for our special music. It was absolutely beautiful!

But the piano and the saxophone are entirely different. There are no strings in a sax as there are in a piano. A piano is not dependent upon wind, as a sax is. You can't hold a piano like you do a sax. You can't place a candelabra upon a sax like you can a piano. They are constructed differently, they look differently, the skills needed to play each is entirely different, and the music they produce is completely different. But they sound beautiful together.

That's how Christians work, too!

Each of us is entirely different. We look different, we sound different, we have different skills, different gifts, different abilities. But we can do some beautiful things together. That's God's plan!

This truth extends beyond the church as well. Around the world people are of different cultures, different colors, different languages, different ethnicities, different customs ... there are all kinds of differences. These differences add strength and beauty to harmonious cooperation, whatever the task at hand.

We are different for a reason. Our differences should not keep us apart; our differences should bring us together! The church is most harmonious when each of us does our part. We can accomplish much more together than we can individually.

The Apostle Paul explained it this way: 1 Corinthians 12:12, "The body is a unit, though it is made up of many parts; and though all its parts are many, they form one body. So it is with Christ."

Just a few verses later he adds, 1 Corinthians 12:18, "But in fact God has arranged the parts in the body, every one of them, just as he wanted them to be."

You are what you are and who you are by God's plan. God's

plan is also that you have a role to play in the church. The church is a stronger church, a healthier church, a more effective church, a more successful church when each of us fulfills our God ordained role in the church.

When church members all use their God given gifts, great things are accomplished and it is indeed something beautiful to behold!

Canyon De Chelly

A few years ago, Lisa and I visited Canyon De Chelly, which is located on the Navajo reservation in Northeast Arizona. (De Chelly is pronounced De-Shay.) Although the area around the canyon is very desolate and barren, (in fact, somewhat boring), the canyon itself is spectacular. We drove both the north and south rim, stopping at several of the observation points. Each observation point gave a different perspective of the canyon. Native American ruins can be seen from several of the points. One of our favorite sites was Spider Rock.

Perhaps the most well-known site in Canyon De Chelly is the White House Indian Ruins. There is a trail that one can hike down into the canyon that takes you to the White House ruins. In fact, it is the only trail that a person can hike in the canyon without hiring a guide. Lisa and I stood at the observation point looking at the trail trying to decide if we would attempt to hike into the canyon. The trail is only about a mile and a half each way, but it goes right down the cliffs to get into the canyon. There are many switchbacks along the trail as it winds into the canyon. It wasn't the hike down that concerned me, it was the hike back up that gave me pause!

We hesitated only briefly and then decided to go for it. It was a beautiful hike! As we descended the trail we stopped several times to appreciate the beauty of God's creation. We took a few pictures, looked at various things along the trail, viewed the canyon from the different levels and before we knew it we had reached our destination. We enjoyed the up close views of the Anasazi ruins and marveled at those who had built them and lived there over 1000 years ago.

After a while we started back up the trail. Again, it was a very enjoyable hike, not difficult at all. We actually made it up the trail in about the same amount of time it took us to go down the trail. My apprehensions about the hike out had been unwarranted.

There are many things in life like that. Unwarranted apprehensions. We worry about things that never happen. We fret about

31

things that are beyond our control. We get anxious about things that turn out much better than we had feared. Our concerns can often rob us of surrounding joyful experiences. We risk getting so wrapped up in unseen fears that we jeopardize completely missing unmistakable blessings.

Jesus said, "Peace I leave with you; my peace I give you. I do not give to you as the world gives. Do not let your hearts be troubled and do not be afraid." John 14:27.

Is it time for you to set some worries, concerns, or fears aside? As you hike the trail of life, don't let worries rob you of the joy of the journey!

Alberto's Patience

"A man's wisdom gives him patience..." Proverbs 19:11.

Over the years we have made many, many trips to Rocky Point, Mexico to build a small home for an underprivileged family there. It's always a joy to get to know the family for whom we are providing a home. One year, after meeting the family, I sat and had a discussion with Alberto, the husband and father of the family.

Using a translator, we had an interesting and informative conversation. Among other things, we discussed the process the family went through to become qualified to receive the house. The thing which really caught my attention was the fact that the family was approved for the home over a year earlier. They've waited an entire year for a decent home to live in. After explaining that to me, there was a slight pause, and then Alberto said something in Spanish. The translator looked at me and said, "Long wait."

Long wait. I looked at Alberto, I looked at his family, I looked at the tiny little house we were building. A house for which they had waited for over a year. Long wait.

Do you ever get impatient? I do. Have you been to a restaurant and the food took longer to get to you than you thought was reasonable? Has someone ever been late for an appointment with you? Have you ever been in a line at a grocery store and the line seemed to move at a snail's pace? Have you ever been stuck in rush hour traffic? Has the foursome in front of you at the golf course seemed to take all day to complete the round? Have you ever gotten anxious because you felt that the preacher's message was a bit too long?

Can you even begin to imagine what it would be like to wait an entire year for a tiny little house for your family?

Long wait? When you look at the big picture, the really important things in life, isn't it silly, even a little embarrassing, at some of the things which try our patience.

Patience: I have a lot of room for improvement in this area! The next time Satan pushes the impatience button on my temptation panel, I'm going to think of Alberto. I have far, far too many blessings in life to let my gratitude be polluted with impatience. How about you?

Galatians 5:22 reads, "The fruit of the Spirit is love, joy, peace, patience...."

Autumn Leaves

For many people, fall is their favorite time of the year. The dropping temperatures give a much anticipated respite from the summer heat. The leaves are changing colors as the foliage takes on a new beauty. And of course, two terrific holidays, Thanksgiving and Christmas, are near. It is certainly understandable why autumn is so popular.

I've always enjoyed seeing the leaves change from green to yellow, orange, and bright red. When our daughters were younger, we'd drive up north just to see the leaves in their multi-colored splendor. It was well worth the drive! A few years ago, Lisa and I took a vacation to the New England states in the fall just to see the brightly colored leaves. Through God's divine plan, the leaves are transformed into a new glory. It is spectacular!

God's divine plan also calls for you to be transformed. The Apostle Paul explained in 2 Corinthians 3:18, "And we, who with unveiled faces all reflect the Lord's glory, are being transformed into his likeness with ever-increasing glory, which comes from the Lord, who is the Spirit."

Wow! For some of us it's hard to imagine such a comparison. It would indeed take an act of God to get us to such a brilliance. As the Apostle explained, it does indeed come from the Lord. It is only by the power of the Lord's indwelling spirit that such a transformation is possible.

Unfortunately, we can "muddy-up" the process by focusing on things of the world instead of focusing on things of the Lord. Paul addresses this as well in Romans 12:2 "Do not conform any longer to the pattern of this world, but be transformed by the renewing of your mind. Then you will be able to test and approve what God's will is - his good, pleasing and perfect will."

What are you putting into your mind? What are you reading? What are you watching? What are you listening to? Who is influencing your life? Prayer, Bible study, worship, Christian fellowship... are all vital ingredients to your metamorphoses.

Be faithful. The end result will be spectacular!

Hidden Treasures

At first I didn't see them, but they were there. A few years ago, we were in Ireland at the Bunratty Castle and surrounding village. While walking the grounds, I happened upon a large pond that was completely surrounded by trees and thick vegetation. It was a beautiful setting: peaceful, tranquil. I found a bench and sat to appreciate a few minutes of silence and solitude.

At first I didn't see them, but they were there. I sat by myself, observing the beauty of the pond: a few lily pads, reeds, various bushes, and trees along the edge of the water. I was there several minutes before I noticed them. A few ducks swimming underneath some overhanging branches of a tree. If I had simply walked past the lake, or only stopped for a minute or two, I never would have seen them, but there they were.

After a couple of minutes, I spotted a few more. They were sitting peacefully on a rock which rose just above the level of the water. A moment later I spied a few more ducks way over on the other side. I watched them for a while, appreciating their beauty and watching their activities. I was glad I had taken the time to look closer at the pond and its inhabitants.

I think that people can sometimes be like that pond. They have "hidden" treasures that are easily missed by casual observation. At first we don't see them, but they are there. It is only when we take the time to get to know them, to observe, to look, to listen, that we begin to discover some of the hidden treasures within each person.

The Psalmist understood this when he wrote, "I praise you because I am fearfully and wonderfully made; your works are wonderful, I know that full well." Psalm 139:14.

Unfortunately, far too often we are so hurried that we simply don't take time to just sit and visit. We have an objective or an agenda in our relationships. There are issues to be addressed. There are problems to be discussed. And so, we hurry on to the next person and the person after that.

If we would only take the time to stop and sit and observe and learn we might very well be surprised at what we discover about those who are all around us. Past experiences, insights, ideas, stories, talents, interests.......at first you might not see them, but they are there, just waiting to be discovered. It's worth the time!

GPS

On a recent trip out of town, Lisa and I relied upon one of those GPS gadgets that many cars are now equipped with. GPS stands for Global Positioning System. To find our hotel, we simply typed in the address of our hotel and the GPS led us right to it. That evening we were going to a restaurant to eat; we input the address and again we were led right to our destination. The next day we wanted to go horseback riding so we put in the address of the nearby stables and before you could say, "Howdy Buckaroo" we were sitting tall in the saddle. Pretty cool!

Even if you don't know the exact address, you can hit the special "Points of Interest" function and it will suggest several locations. So long as you know where you want to go and you are willing to follow the directions, it will lead you to your desired location.

Wouldn't it be great if such a system existed for everyday life?! Guess what? Such a system does exist! I call it GPS: God's Positioning System. You start by making sure you are equipped with a Bible. Through prayer you send a signal to the Lord in heaven who is tracking your location. Via the presence of the Holy Spirit you will be directed in the way you ought to go. Before you can say, "Hallelujah Jesus!" you'll be led to your destination. You will ultimately get where you need to be and will be blessed with many "Points of Interest" along the way.

The Psalmist wrote, "O Lord, you have searched me and you know me. You know when I sit and when I rise; you perceive my thoughts from afar. You discern my going out and my lying down; you are familiar with all my ways." Psalm 139:1-3.

Isaiah 48:17 says, "This is what the Lord says - your Redeemer, the Holy One of Israel: 'I am the Lord your God, who teaches you what is best for you, who directs you in the way you should go.'"

The best feature of this GPS is the "Eternity" function. Of course, you first have to determine where you want to go for eternity.

And then, and here's the critical part, you have to be willing to follow the proper directions. Following the wrong directions will cause you to become lost. You don't want that to happen. But if you follow the directions from God's Positioning System, paradise is guaranteed!

Exodus 15:13, "In your unfailing love you will lead the people you have redeemed. In your strength you will guide them to your holy dwelling."

Wherever you go, make sure you go with God!

Heavenly!

Lake Tahoe is one of God's beautiful creations here on earth. While visiting there, Lisa and I took a gondola ride to the top of the Heavenly Ski Resort. The ride itself is spectacular and the views at the observation deck will take your breath away.

The gondola takes you 2.5 miles up the side of a mountain with an altitude gain of approximately 3,000 feet. There are 35 massive towers which hold the cables for the gondolas. It is estimated that it took 48,000 man hours to build the entire project. The Heavenly mountain top experience, awesome views, an amazing location... all available to me with virtually no effort on my part. I didn't have to build the towers or run the cable or clear a path through the forest. I didn't have to hike to the top of the mountain. I was able to get to the top of the mountain simply by paying a fee and stepping into the gondola. What a deal!

Of course, the name "Heavenly Ski Resort" conjures up thoughts of Heaven itself. While the owners of the resort were focused on the "Heavenly" views and inspirational location while selecting the celestial identity, I think there is something even more divine than they may have realized.

The gondola ride to the top and our future ascent to Heaven have much in common. No doubt it will be a spectacular ride and the first glimpse of Heaven will take your breath away. The ride is available with no work required on your part. The fee has already been paid! The fact that the trip is even possible is no small feat. Instead of 35 massive towers there was one ominous cross. Instead of dozens of men working some 48,000 man hours, there is the One and Only Jesus Christ: "The Way, The Truth and The Life." At the top of the mountain we heard tourists speaking different languages. All nationalities, races, and ethnicities are welcome to ride the gondola. Likewise, the Bible says that "Everyone who calls upon the name of the Lord will be saved." Romans 10:13.

If you want to reach the ETERNAL Heavenly resort, there is only one way to get there.   "Salvation is found in no one else, for there is no other name under heaven given to men by which we must be saved." Acts 4:12.

The gondola provided the way to an enjoyable afternoon. Jesus Christ provides the only way to an incredible eternity of joyous celebration.

His is the true Heavenly experience!

Jury Duty

I received the summons in the mail: Jury Duty! I've received the notice before and made my obligatory visit to the court, spending the day going through the selection process. But that is as far as it has ever gone. I'd never been selected. Until now. By the end of the day I was one of the "lucky" ones chosen to sit on the jury.

I didn't mind. Our country is a great country for many reasons, one of which is our judicial system. In order for it to work, someone needs to be on the jury. It was my turn, so I was willing to serve my civic duty.

It really was an informative and interesting process. Evidence was submitted. Witnesses were questioned. Arguments were made. By Thursday afternoon we began our jury deliberation. I thought it would be over quickly, a couple of hours and we'd be headed home. I was wrong. We deliberated all afternoon Thursday and returned Friday morning to continue. We did reach our decision by midday Friday and reported to the Judge and the court: Guilty, on all three counts.

The entire experience reminded me of a Biblical truth. The defendant denied any wrong doing.   But the evidence proved otherwise. The Bible teaches, "...you may be sure that your sin will find you out." Numbers 32:23.

We may be able to hide our sins for now, we may be able to keep our little secrets for a while, but eventually, we will all have our day of judgement. "Therefore judge nothing before the appointed time; wait till the Lord comes. He will bring to light what is hidden in darkness and will expose the motives of men's hearts...." 1 Corinthians 4:5.

The fact of the matter is, we all have made our mistakes, we've all done something wrong, we've all sinned....and thus, we all deserve condemnation. But that's where the story abruptly changes. Jesus steps in and assumes our penalty. He serves our time. He takes our punishment. That's what the cross was all about. As a result, we don't receive the sentencing that we deserve.

Isaiah prophesied this truth about Jesus, "He was pierced for our transgressions, he was crushed for our iniquities; the punishment that brought us peace was upon him, and by his wounds we are healed." Isaiah 53:5.

That's why the Apostle Paul wrote, "Therefore, there is now no condemnation for those who are in Christ Jesus." Romans 8:1.

Instead of being thrown in jail, or worse, we are set free. "It is for freedom that Christ has set us free..." Galatians 5:1.

God is a second chance God. We've been given a new lease on life! Let us appreciate our freedom and use our time wisely. Let us thank our Righteous Judge for His tremendous grace and mercy.

Pelicans

Late one Spring, I was in Rocky Point, Mexico. One afternoon I took a long walk along the beach. There's something therapeutic about watching the waves roll up onto the shore. I think it is similar to staring into a campfire. It can be mesmerizing and very relaxing.

As I walked along the beach, waves rising from ankles to knees, I was intrigued by the various birds: Sandpipers, seagulls, pelicans... some bobbing up and down in the water, some running along the beach, some floating along the wind currents.

A flock of pelicans graciously glided along the surface of the water, their wing tips occasionally dipping into the water as they slowly flew past me. A few minutes later, two or three pelicans seemed to be suspended in air as they faced the wind; adjusting their wings with the air currents, they seemed to barely move as they scanned the water below them. They were fishing. Eventually, one folded his wings back against his body and dove straight down into the water to catch a fish in it's large beak. It then sat, bobbing with the surge of the sea, as it digested it's food.

This ritual was repeated over and over as more pelicans and other birds did their own fishing.   Although it was not their intention, they put on a great show for me.   And though I had seen this routine before, I still found it fascinating. What remarkable creatures! They can walk on land, they can fly, they can float on top of water, they can dive into water. They have an abundant supply of food at their disposable. What a life. For centuries God has taken care of such birds.

I am reminded of the words of Jesus, "Look at the birds of the air; they do not sow or reap or store away in barns, and yet your heavenly Father feeds them. Are you not much more valuable than they?" Matthew 6:26.

Pelicans are more than entertaining. From them we are reminded of God's intimate involvement in our lives. He provides ways for us to have food, water, shelter and other essentials in life. Being aware of God's presence is a great source of peace. As peaceful as a walk along the beach, waves nipping at your ankles, pelicans gliding by...

Stuck In Traffic

They called it a "buffalo jam." In the city we have traffic jams. But in Yellowstone Park, they have buffalo jams. The narrow two lane road was bumper to bumper with cars. A buffalo had decided to lie down right next to the road for a little rest. Cars driving by slowed to a crawl or stopped completely to snap a picture. It wasn't long until the traffic jam, er ah, I mean, buffalo jam, stretched back more than a mile.

This stop-and-go slow down wasn't caused by a traffic accident or road construction. We weren't staring at buildings and concrete and asphalt.   And we weren't in sweltering Arizona summer heat. As we inched along, we enjoyed beautiful meadows, majestic mountains, stately pine trees... and eventually, a buffalo. Besides that, we were on vacation, so what's the hurry anyways?

The Lord spoke to the psalmist and said, "Be still and know that I am God." Psalm 46:10.

Long traffic lights, accidents on the freeway, road construction, and other things sometimes force us to "be still." But we aren't really still, are we?   Are we going to miss the appointment, will we be late for dinner, is the one waiting for us going to be mad? The pulse rate quickens, the nerves tighten, the mind whirls, the knuckles whiten, the anxiety level climbs... not at all what the Lord had in mind when he said to "be still."

In Phoenix, I absolutely HATE being in a traffic jam. In Yellowstone, it didn't bother me much at all. I suppose location is the key. Perhaps remembering our spiritual location is also the key. How quickly we forget that we are in Christ.

Jesus said, "I have told you these things, so that in me you may have peace. In this world you will have trouble. But take heart! I have overcome the world." John 16:33.

Buffalo or buildings, meadows or asphalt, trees or traffic... the

47

scenery always changes. But our location doesn't have to change. Jesus said, "...And surely I am with you always, to the very end of the age." Matthew 28:20.

How's your location?

African Safari

God's incredible design can be clearly seen in that which He created. This was seen over and over again while on our safari in Africa. We saw a crocodile sitting on the bank of a small watering hole. The croc had his mouth wide open. A small bird was IN it's mouth, picking at it's teeth. The bird actually cleans the teeth of the croc. Why doesn't the croc close it's mouth and swallow the bird? Because crocodiles don't like feathers! The bird gets a free meal and the croc gets it's teeth cleaned. It's called a symbiotic relationship.

The hippopotamus spends most of the day submerged in water because it's skin is sensitive to the sun. At night it forages for food and returns to the water as the sun rises. Unfortunately, while grazing, many tics and bugs climb onto the hippo. To keep from drowning, these bugs climb to the "high point" of the hippo, usually the ridge of his back or the top of his head, once it returns to the water. The local birds then land on the hippo for a smorgasbord of their favorite bugs!

We saw several giraffes feeding among the trees. They consume a large quantity of leaves. If they were to strip the tree of all of it's leaves, it might very well kill the tree. However, after several minutes of being nibbled upon, the tree secretes a certain chemical which is distasteful to the giraffe. So, after a few minutes at one tree the giraffe will move on to the next tree, and the first tree still has most of it's leaves intact.

The various patterns of colors on the animals serve to help camouflage them from predators.

When two or more rhinoceroses lie down, they will ALWAYS face opposite directions, so as to watch for predators.

We saw these and many, many more examples of God's handiwork. God has "programmed" these animals and plants so that they can survive in the wilds of Africa. They are a living testimony of God's existence and His compassion, concern, and provision for all of

His creation.

The Apostle Paul wrote, "For since the creation of the world God's invisible qualities — His eternal power and divine nature — have been clearly seen, being understood from what has been made, so that men are without excuse." Romans 1:20.

Since creation itself, God has been intimately involved in that which He created. The evidence is all around us!

Contagious!

Four generations. All here at church. Nearly every Sunday. Faith is contagious. You catch it from those who are closest to you.

We see them regularly on Sunday morning: Addy and her brother, Brody. The unique thing about these children is that they are typically at church Sunday morning with their mom, Ashley and step-dad Marc, their grandma Tammy, and their great grandma Betty and great grandpa Boyd. Additionally, extended family members such as Aunt Brittany and Uncle Ross and other great uncles and aunts are there, too! Four generations. All in church.

Where do children learn to be faithful in worship? They learn it from their parents. We hear a lot about peer pressure. Peer pressure notwithstanding, the number one influence on a young child's life is still their family. That begins with parents and certainly includes grandparents. Moms and dads, grandmas and grandpas all set a living example of faith for their children and grandchildren. Older siblings and uncles and aunts also have their fair share of influence.

The Apostle Paul wrote to Timothy, "I have been reminded of your sincere faith, which first lived in your grandmother Lois and in your mother Eunice and, I am persuaded, now lives in you also." 2 Timothy 1:5.

Peer pressure is a reality that children and their parents have to deal with while children are growing up. Of course, depending on who those peers are determines whether peer pressure is a bad thing or a good thing in children's lives. Making sure your children are involved in Sunday School and other of the church's children and youth programs and activities certainly increases the chance of peer pressure being a positive, instead of a negative, influence.

Proverbs 22:6 says, "Train a child in the way he should go, and when he is old he will not turn from it."

On Sunday morning there is much more than worship going on: lives are being shaped! You are setting an example of faithfulness in worship for the next generation.

Faith is contagious. You catch it from those who are closest to you!

Tourist Attractions

Here in Arizona, halfway between the towns of Prescott and Sedona, is the small town of Clarksville. At Clarksville, one can find the depot for the Verde Canyon Railroad. We boarded the train and began the journey up the Verde Canyon. Although the surrounding mountains are somewhat barren, there is a lush green riparian area which follows the river. Our train traversed several canyons, crossing on old wooden bridges supported by a network of trestles. It also passed through a 680-foot-long tunnel that curved through the mountain.

At one time the train was used as a major means of transportation in that part of the state, especially to and from the mining towns along the Verde Canyon. Nowadays the train is only used as a tourist attraction. It has long ceased to function for its original purpose.

A few years ago, while in Europe, I visited many, many church cathedrals. With their magnificent architecture, dazzling interior decor, priceless artwork, and spectacular stained glass windows, they are absolutely beautiful to behold. However, many of them no longer house congregations or hold any worship services. Nowadays, they only serve as a tourist attraction. They have long ceased to function for their original purpose.

What is the original purpose of the church? Have we become nothing more than a spiritual tourist attraction? Nothing more than a religious social club?

The fact is, the church is multifaceted in its purpose. At the top of the list, Jesus Himself established the reason for our existence when He said, "Therefore go make disciples of all nations, baptizing them in the name of the Father and of the Son and of the Holy Spirit." Matthew 28:19.

Nothing touristy about that. We've got a job to do! We are to enthusiastically and passionately share Jesus Christ with the rest of the world. And while we are reaching out compassionately to others, let's not forget about one another. Jesus also said, "A new command I give you: Love one another. As I have loved you, so you must love one another." John 13:34.

Simply stated, the purpose of the church is to love one another and to share the love of Christ with others around the world. Now, that's a purpose for existence that's worth hanging on to.

All aboard!

F-18 Flight Simulator

Recently I was in Seattle, Washington, and took some time to visit the airplane museum at Boeing. They have an entire room filled with World War I airplanes. Another room is filled with World War II planes. They have a room with a variety of space "planes": everything from a Gemini space capsule to the lunar lander to a replica of a section of the space station.

Their main room has all kinds of planes, some hanging from the ceiling, others spread around the floor; it's a very large room! Truth be told, I'm just a little boy trapped inside an old man's body. I was in hog heaven.

If you've got the nerve, you can even take a spin in an F-18 flight simulator. We had the nerve, so we took our turn. Chad Pace and I crawled into the tandem simulator. After brief instructions, the hatch was locked and we, "took off."

In addition to a large simulation screen directly in front of you, the simulator itself has 360-degree axis rotation. That means if you turn the plane upside down in simulation, you will be literally hanging upside down in the simulator.

I took the controls first. (Being the boss has its privileges.) When my time had expired Chad took the controls. Being a real pilot, he was anxious to "see what this baby will do." He immediately decided to "buzz the tower." Of course, he did so upside down at full throttle. He then cranked it sideways and began to climb, as he said, "Let's see how many G's we can pull." After several loops, spins, and other wild maneuvers, our time came to an end. What a blast!

You know what? Life really is a blast. Unfortunately, far too many individuals view life through a simulator; a.k.a. their television. With the plethora of reality shows which are so popular, viewers settle for vicarious living. They've settled for a simulation instead of the real thing.

In the Gospel of John 10:10, Jesus said, "...I came that they might have life, and might have it abundantly." NASB.

Don't be deceived, coach potato living is not abundant life living. There's a great big beautiful world out there just waiting to be enjoyed. Mountains, lakes, oceans, rivers, parks, adventures, airplanes, boats, trains, places, people, things... God has blessed us with an incredible life.

Now, get up off that couch! Let's go out, praise God, and let's see how many G's we can pull!!

Sedona Hike

While visiting the beautiful town of Sedona, we decided to get up early in the morning to hike the Faye Canyon trail. As we hiked along the trail, we passed two guys from out of state who were fascinated by a rattlesnake they found along the edge of the trail. They were standing just a few feet away from it taking pictures. After warning them of how quickly the snake could strike, we continued along our journey.

The trail had only a very slight grade as we followed a dry stream bed up the canyon. Eventually we left the main trail, crossed the stream to a narrower trail, and began our ascent up the side of a mountain. Our hike quickly became much more difficult, requiring several stops to catch our breath. Before long we had reached our destination: The Faye Canyon Arch. We stood under the arch and looked up at a few petroglyphs, reminders of an ancient civilization. From our vantage point we had a tremendous view of the beautiful Sedona area.

Our little hike reminded me of life's journey. Some parts of the journey are easy, some are much more strenuous. Sometimes you need a little break just to catch your breath. Sunday morning worship and midweek Bible study groups provide such a break. The snake, symbolic of satan, lies along the edge of the trail waiting to divert you from your destination. Satan is able to strike quickly when least expected. Be very careful as you pass by the dwelling places of the serpent.

To reach the mountain top, symbolic of heaven, you have to leave the wide trail and take a path less traveled. Jesus said, "...broad is the road that leads to destruction... narrow the road that leads to life, and only a few find it." Matthew 7:13-14.

Once the summit has been reached, we will be reminded that many of God's faithful have been there before us. The Apostle Paul reminds of this when he writes, "Therefore, since we are surrounded by such a great cloud of witnesses, let us throw off everything that hinders and the sin that so easily entangles, and let us run with perseverance the race marked out for us." Hebrews 12:1.

Where are you on life's journey? Each Sunday faithful Christians around the world gather to "catch our breath," praise and worship the creator of our path, encourage fellow travelers, check our map to be sure we're on the right trail, and then continue our journey to the summit. Will you join us?

Bougainvillea

We have a couple of large bougainvillea plants on the front of our house. They have been trained to climb the trellis that covers the entire two stories above the flower box where they are planted. Their bright pink and red flowers bloom year round. The flowers, and the bright green leaves behind them, are usually very pretty.

I say usually, because there have been times when they were, in fact, extremely ugly. On more than one occasion over the years, a deep winter freeze froze our mighty bougainvillea. The pink and red flowers had withered and fallen to the ground. The fresh, bright green leaves became a wrinkled, dingy brown. On such occasions, the plants look dead.

But then comes spring. We've learned what it takes to save our beautiful bougainvillea. As the weather warms and the sun shines on the plant, it will begin to recover. I'll trim away the dead branches, we'll faithfully water it, and the sun will do the rest.

The same is true for us Christians. Sometimes our spiritual life seems to go through a dead spell. There's no excitement in our worship time. There's no compassion in our fellowship. There's no enthusiasm in our witnessing. Someone once referred to Christians at such a time as the, "chosen frozen."

How does one recover? Exposure to the Son! Jesus said, "I am the vine, you are the branches. If a man remains in me and I in him, he will bear much fruit; apart from me you can do nothing." John 15:5.

Jesus also said that His Father will prune the branches. "I am the true vine, and my Father is the gardener. He cuts off every branch in me that bears no fruit, while every branch that does bear fruit he prunes so that it will be even more fruitful." John 15:1-3.

Do you feel guilty, or convicted, when you've done something wrong? Is there some "dead wood" in your life the Lord needs to trim away? You will be more fruitful if you allow your Heavenly Father to do some gardening in your life.

Does your soul need to be watered? Jesus said, "...If anyone is thirsty, let him come to me and drink. Whoever believes in me, as the Scripture has said, streams of living water will flow from within him." John 7:37-38.

Life giving spiritual growth is in abundance as you bask in the warmth of the divine and water your soul. Sunday morning worship is a good place to receive a healthy exposure to the Son! Let the renewal and growth begin!

Eating in Peru

While in Peru on a short-term mission trip, I tried some foods which I had never before tasted. The first was ceviche. Ceviche is raw fish which has been marinated in lemon or lime juice. The acidic quality of the juice sears the fish and takes the place of actually cooking it. To my surprise, it was delicious! I had it several times.

The next new meal I tried was alpaca meat. An alpaca is similar to a llama, only slightly smaller. It is raised for it's fur and it's meat. Eating the meat reminded me of eating a very thin porkchop. However, the porkchop tastes much better!

My final new culinary experience was the consumption of cuy (pronounced gwe). In America we refer to it as guinea pig. I was told it was a delicacy of the Incan Kings. To my astonishment, when our food was served, the entire animal was on my plate. Everything was still intact: Head, tail, legs, feet, claws, buck teeth... everything! There just isn't very much meat on the little critter. I would compare the taste to that of the dark brown meat of a turkey. Although the taste was tolerable, the presentation tended to minimize one's hunger. No wonder the Incan Kings are no longer in existence!

I must admit, I was very happy to get back home and sink my teeth into a good ol' cheeseburger. Think about a simple cheeseburger, what a wonderful thing. I think that I shall never take a cheeseburger for granted again! Those poor Incan Kings just didn't know what they were missing.

Not only did the meals of Peru deepen my appreciation of a cheeseburger, the lack of meals for many convicted me to a new level of gratitude. As we walked among the barrios we were reminded again that providing food for the family was a daily challenge. Food is not a given among the world's poor. And having choices as to what to eat is rare indeed.

The Apostle Paul wrote, "Give thanks in all circumstances..." 1 Thessalonians 5:18

We are blessed. Tremendously. Let us be generous. It really doesn't take much to make a big difference in the lives of many around the world.

Jesus said, "I was hungry and you gave me something to eat, I was thirsty and you gave me something to drink, I was a stranger and you invited me in, I needed clothes and you clothed me, I was sick and you looked after me, I was in prison and you came to visit me.'" He then added, "...Whatever you did for one of the least of these brothers of mine, you did for me." Matthew 25:35-36, 40.

Let us be generous. Let us also be thankful. Even for the little things we tend to take for granted, like a cheeseburger!

Pebble Beach

The Pebble Beach Golf Course is considered by many to be the number one golf course in the world. Located along the Pacific Ocean in beautiful Monterey, California, it has breathtaking views as it winds its way along the cliffs of the Monterey Peninsula. An occasional deer can be seen grazing on the fairway as seagulls fly overhead. Any hack who has ever picked up a golf club has dreamed about playing at Pebble Beach. Dreams do come true!

A few years ago, eight of us made our way up to northern California to play the famed course. We walked the same fairways as Jack Nicklaus and Arnold Palmer. We putted on the same greens as Tiger Woods and Phil Mickelson. We hit errant shots into the same ocean as David Duval and Sergio Garcia. We played golf at Pebble Beach!

I was more than a little nervous as I teed up my ball on that first tee. My mind was flooded with the history of the course, the crowd watching, the video camera rolling. True to form, I shanked my first drive into a neighboring back yard! (Praise God for Mulligans!)

To maximize the experience, we hired a caddy and walked the entire 18 holes. In my mind, the course lived up to all the hype. There was no let down. I loved it!

Do you ever dream about Heaven? I do. I wonder what it's going to be like. If places on earth can be as incredibly beautiful as the Monterey Peninsula, how spectacular will Heaven be? What will it be like to walk along with King David and Elijah? How incredible to look up and see angels floating nearby. What an experience to sit and converse with the Apostle Peter and Mary, the mother of Jesus. Dreams do come true!

No Mulligans will be needed in heaven. For the Lord has already washed away all of our "errant shots." The fees have already been paid, the transportation has been arranged, our place has been reserved. The best part is, we will not be limited to 18 holes or even limited to 18 thousand years. We will experience Heaven for all of eternity!

To maximize the experience, we'll be in the presence of the Lord, Himself. Not because we are worthy or we deserve it or we are good enough. Simply because He loves us and because of His incredible grace.

Jesus said, "In my Father's house are many rooms; if it were not so, I would have told you. I am going there to prepare a place for you. And if I go and prepare a place for you, I will come back and take you to be with me that you also may be where I am." (John 14:2-3)

Amen, come Lord Jesus.

Mowing The Lawn

My lawnmower was broken. The engine just wouldn't start. I tried the usual things to make it work: Make sure there's enough gas in the tank... change the spark plug... clean the air filter ... nothing seemed to work. So, I hauled it to a lawnmower shop to get it fixed.

Meanwhile, the grass in the back yard continued to grow. It was already due to be mowed when the mower broke down. Then it took me a few days to find a repair shop and get it to the shop. They had it for a week doing their repairs. Meanwhile the grass continued to grow. The rains helped it grow even faster than normal. By the time I got the lawn mower back and could get to mowing the lawn, the grass was ankle deep. I could have used a hay baler to do the job! The simple task of mowing the yard became a big job.

It's amazing how little neglected things can grow into big things in your life if not dealt with in a timely fashion. A little argument with a friend becomes a big issue if not resolved appropriately. A little disagreement with your spouse becomes bigger than necessary if not resolved in a loving way. Resentment toward a family member for a little wrong can fester and grow if not dealt with in a healthy way.

Neglect of daily devotions and prayer time becomes the norm rather than the exception when allowed to occur for too long. Even missing church a few Sundays can create an awkwardness in returning to where you should be.

The Apostle Paul encouraged, "Let us not become weary in doing good, for at the proper time we will reap a harvest if we do not give up." Galatians 6:9.

I did eventually get the grass mowed. It took longer and was more a challenge that first time. However, so long as I mow each week, it's not difficult at all.

The Psalmist said to the Lord, "I will hasten and not delay to obey your commands." Psalm 119:60.

Is there something you have neglected to do in your life? A

strained relationship, a neglected responsibility, a healthy routine...?
The longer you wait, the worse it gets. The quicker you deal with it, the easier the following weeks and months will be.

Just like mowing the lawn.

Rafting The Rapids!

My wife Lisa, my daughter Michelle and I were white water rafting near Fort Collins, Colorado. We rafted 8 miles on the Poudre river. What a ride! There were six in our raft, including the guide. We made it through several challenging rapids, and also enjoyed short stretches of calmer waters. The guide did a masterful job of guiding us around the protruding boulders. We survived the ride because we faithfully followed the instructions of the guide.

Halfway through the rapids, the front of the raft caught a submerged rock. If we had seen it, we could have avoided it. But we didn't and now the current was swinging the raft sideways. Before we knew it, we had swung all the way around and were facing upstream. The guide gave the command, "paddle backwards." We slid off the rock, but now we proceeded down the rapids backward. She gave another command, "right side paddle forward, left side paddle backward." Very quickly the raft swung around and we proceeded down the rapids, front first.

The guide continued to bark out instructions and we successfully traversed the rapids which had been appropriately named "Pinball" because of the many boulders which bounced the raft down the river.

Life can be like rafting down a river. The years roll by, like currents carrying you downstream. Challenges in life stick out like boulders, which must be maneuvered as one continues on the journey. In our raft are family members and friends who can help us successfully overcome the rapids and share the beauty and joy of calmer waters.

And of course there is our guide. Not only will He direct us in our journey, but He will make sure we reach our ultimate destination. Jesus said, "If anyone would come after me, he must deny himself and take up his cross, and follow me." (Matthew 16:24)

The key to surviving the challenges in life is to follow life's guide, Jesus. He can guide you on an exhilarating journey. What a ride!

The Lost Key

Lisa and I, along with Lisa's sister and brother-in-law, Sherry and Don, had chartered a forty-four-foot yacht and were snorkeling off the coast of the Isla Mujeres, just north of Cancun, Mexico. The water was unbelievably clear and an amazing variety of turquoise, aqua and other various shades of beautiful blue colors. We saw many, many brightly colored fish swimming among the reef.

We were having a wonderful time ... but then it happened! We could see a key slowing falling to the bottom of the ocean floor. A key with a blue cord on it. A key that came to rest approximately thirty-five feet below us. A key which could be clearly seen from the surface of the water, but was too deep to retrieve. A key which I had forgotten to remove from my swimming suit pocket before jumping into the water.

The key to my room!

Now what do we do? Our key was at the bottom of a watery grave. Would we be locked out of our room? How would we get in? Would we be forced to spend the night in the darkness on some lonely, uncomfortable park bench?

Fortunately, we had another key and had no trouble getting into our room.

Many assume that death is a permanent situation, as if they have been "locked out" of life. But that is not necessarily the case. Did you know that there is a key that unlocks the doors of death? And who do you think holds that key? You guessed it, Jesus Christ.

Look at Revelation 1:17-18, "...Then he placed his right hand on me and said: "Do not be afraid. I am the First and the Last. I am the Living One; I was dead, and behold I am alive for ever and ever! And I hold the keys of death and Hades."

Death is not permanent! We will not be locked in a grave for eternity. There is a key which will set us free. That key has not been lost.

But please understand, there are no spare keys to the doors of death. Jesus Christ holds the one and only key. Jesus Christ is the only one who can open the doors of death. Jesus Christ is the only one who can open the doors of heaven. Jesus Christ is THE key to your eternal salvation.

Aren't you glad THAT key is in safe hands!

The Climb

As you approach the little town of Strawberry, Arizona, there is a trail off the right side of the highway. It is called the Rim View Trail. It begins with a steep ascent, following an old wagon trail up the face of the mountain. It winds its way up the hill and eventually reaches the top of the mountain. It then traverses the mountain top and eventually runs parallel to the Mogollon Rim. (Locals will tell you, Mogollon is pronounced "Muggy-yawn.")

It's a strenuous hike but incredibly beautiful as you wind your way through the forest. After about three miles of hiking, I took a side trail to the edge of the rim and found a rock to sit on for a while. The view was spectacular! Tall ponderosa pine trees, massive boulders, views unencumbered by any sign of civilization. It truly was breathtaking.

In order to appreciate the view, one must first make the climb. Isn't that true in most areas of our life? It's called paying your dues. Others would say, "No pain, no gain." Athletes who reach the pinnacle of their sport have been committed to their workouts and exercises. Musicians who are at the top of their field spend hours and hours in practice and rehearsals. Business executives who have reached the peak of their profession have put in the hours of hard work to advance in their careers.

The spiritual journey is no different. Jesus calls us to diligence when he said, "As long as it is day, we must do the work of him who sent me. Night is coming, when no one can work." John 9:4.

The Apostle Paul's understanding of this is seen when he wrote, "Everyone who competes in the games goes into strict training. They do it to get a crown that will not last; but we do it to get a crown that will last forever." 1 Corinthians 9:25.

In order to appreciate the view, one must first make the climb.

Are you making the climb toward that spiritual summit? Are you diligent in prayer, Bible study, worship, service? The good news is, you're not alone as you make the climb. Other travelers are on the same path.

Let's help each other reach the summit!

Ashes

Ashes were everywhere. They covered the surface of the swimming pool. You could see them on sidewalks and driveways. The cars were blanketed in ashes. The ashes were the fallout from the Cave Creek fire. Several mornings in a row, the wind blew south. Our town of Fountain Hills was covered in smoke. The stench was so strong it made one wonder if a new fire, much closer to town, had broken out. Then the wind shifted and the smoke blew away, leaving ashes everywhere.   The smoke was gone, but the ashes remained.

Sin has its own fallout. It leaves scarred lives and broken hearts. Sometimes the fallout from sin covers many lives. Its stench lingers long after the sin has blown away. Long after the temporary pleasure of sin is gone, the consequences of sin remains.

Hundreds of firefighters had gathered to help battle the raging inferno north of town. They saved the homes in that area, and elsewhere. Their goal was to keep the fire from spreading. They wanted to put it out!

The church is here to help you battle the temptations of sin. The truth is, we have indeed saved many homes from sin's devastation. Our goal is to keep sin from spreading. We want to put an end to sin!

The ashes from the fire can easily be washed away. A car wash or a garden hose can get the job done.

Sin's residue can be washed away, too. The blood of Jesus Christ and the waters of baptism can get the job done.

1 Corinthians 6:11 "...You were washed, you were sanctified, you were justified in the name of the Lord Jesus Christ and by the Spirit of our God."

Acts 22:16 "And now what are you waiting for? Get up, be baptized and wash your sins away, calling on his name."

Are you covered with the vestige of sin? You don't have to live under the ashes! Let the cleansing waters of Christian baptism, a life lived in Christ and the fellowship of the church freshen your life.

World War II Bombers

I'll let you in on a little secret: There's a little boy trapped inside this old man's body. Like all little boys, I like airplanes, boats, trains, tractors, bulldozers, motorcycles, rockets... just about anything mechanical with an engine. Thus my ears perked up when I heard on the news that two airplanes, a B-17 Flying Fortress and a B-24 Liberator, were on display at Falcon Field Airport. When the reporter said that visitors could crawl around inside of the planes, I was on my way!

The restored World War II bombers were, as little kids would say, awesome! We had a heyday walking around the planes, crawling through the planes, checking out the bomb-bay doors, standing at the gunner's turret, looking at the navigator's seat.

I asked one of the crew if I could take it for a test spin. He smiled and said, "Maybe next time." No matter how much you crawl around a plane, as fun as that is, it's just not the same as flying in one.

Many people experience Christianity the same way. They see it on display on Sunday morning and they rush over and check it out. They sing the songs, take communion, pray, make a contribution, and listen to the sermon. They go home with a great experience but not really having taken flight. Being at church on Sunday morning is essential for the true Christian. It's like an airport for an airplane. However, no matter how much you crawl around Christianity on Sunday morning, as fun and as important as that is, it's just not the same as soaring with Christ during the week.

The Apostle Paul wrote, "So then, just as you received Christ Jesus as Lord, continue to live in Him." Colossians 2:6.

Airplanes are meant to fly! They need airports, but their true purpose is fulfilled while away from airports. Christians are meant to "Let your light shine," and to be "salt and light" and to "walk in Him."

That adventure happens during the week. It happens in your neighborhoods, where you work, at family gatherings, at the park... it happens Monday through Saturday. We need to gather for worship on Sunday, but a big part of our purpose happens away from the Sunday morning experience.

In the Book of Revelation, Jesus encouraged the church at Ephesus to, "Remember the height from which you have fallen!" Revelation 2:5.

Are you soaring with the Lord? Or has your faith been grounded? Be sure to join other Christians on Sunday morning as we fuel up the tank, check out the flaps, and head down the runway. But then, get ready for takeoff! The Lord will have you soaring in no time at all!

A Rope Swing

We were on a wilderness adventure while visiting the Hawaiian Island of Kauai. The adventure began with a two-mile kayak trip up a river and a hike in a tropical rain forest. Eventually we hiked down a short trail which led to a dazzling waterfall. Below the cascading falls was a large beautiful lagoon. Looking across the lagoon we saw it: A large tree perched on the edge of a cliff overlooking the lagoon. High in its branches was a rope swing. The word "adventure" suddenly took on a whole new meaning!

To get to the tree we had to swim across the lagoon (upstream), climb a 25-foot extension ladder, scamper up some rocks around the tree, and then stand on a perch overlooking the lagoon. While standing there the guide explained, "Don't let go of the rope too soon or you'll go straight down and break your legs in the shallow water. And don't panic and forget to let go of the rope or you'll slam against the cliff when you swing back. Other than that, have fun."

He explained that it was about a 35 foot drop into the lagoon, assuming you let go at the right time. I grabbed the rope, took one last look at my beautiful wife who stood on the other side of the lagoon, and swung. Yippee! AAAAaaaaa. Splash. What a blast! It was indeed an exhilarating adventure. The key was letting go at the right time.

Letting go is also a key element of one's faith. Trusting God with the critical areas of your life is, ultimately, an act of letting go. Letting go of self and living completely for Christ is what it's all about.

Galatians 2:20, "I have been crucified with Christ and I no longer live, but Christ lives in me. The life I live in the body, I live by faith in the Son of God, who loved me and gave himself for me."

Trusting the Lord is a leap of faith. When you do, it is indeed an exhilarating experience. Trusting him to guide you into different areas of ministry can be a real adventure.

Proverbs 3:5-6, "Trust in the LORD with all your heart and lean not on your own understanding; in all your ways acknowledge him, and he will make your paths straight."

Is it time for you to let go and take the plunge? What new adventure might the Lord have in store for you? Grab the rope, step out on faith, and let the adventure begin!

Thanksgiving Dinner

Why did I eat so much for Thanksgiving?! Turkey, mashed potatoes and gravy, stuffing, green beans, ham, lemon bread, buttered rolls... my plate was maxed out. I really didn't need a second helping. But the food was sooooo good that I couldn't control myself. I went back for another plateful. I ate so much I ached. What a glutton!

After eating we went for a walk. (Or should I say we went for a waddle.) The only reason I went on the walk was to make room for dessert. I love dessert! We had several choices: pumpkin pie with whipped cream, pecan pie, cheesecake covered with cherries, and peanut butter fudge bars. I had one of each. I'll have to diet for most of next year to lose the weight I gained from that one meal.

Why do we do it? Why do we indulge in things that we know we will regret the very next day? Why do we give into temptation? Why don't we have more willpower? Whether it's the sin of gluttony, or gossip, or prejudice, or materialism, or any other sin, why do we sometimes give in? We can relate with the Apostle Paul who said, "For what I do is not the good I want to do; no, the evil I do not want to do-this I keep on doing." Romans 7:19.

Of course, satan is no dummy. He makes sin look delicious, pleasurable, desirable, gratifying... he makes it look fun. What is the key, then, to resisting sin?

As Paul explained a few verses later in Romans 7, Jesus is the key. "Thanks be to God - through Jesus Christ our Lord!" Romans 7:25.

Later, in 1 Corinthians 15:57, Paul states, "But thanks be to God, He gives us the victory through our Lord Jesus Christ."

On my own I simply can't resist the temptations of most sins. But with the Lord's help, through the power of Jesus Christ and the presence of His Holy Spirit, I can be victorious.

How about you? What's your sin? Do you give in more often than you'd like to admit? Are you tired of letting satan have his way with you? Eat your meal with Jesus. Go shopping with Jesus. Watch

TV with Jesus. Include Jesus in your conversations with others. Jesus is the key to victory over sin.

Now, Jesus, about that peanut butter fudge...

My Pedometer

It's called a pedometer. It's supposed to measure the distance you walk. Lisa purchased one for me recently. We like to hike and I thought it would be fun to see just how far we have gone on our various excursions. I was anxious to get the thing calibrated to my stride and begin measuring our distances. Seems easy enough to do, right? Wrong!

You see, this is no ordinary pedometer. This one has the capacity to measure and record seven different trips. It has the capacity of breaking each of these trips down into smaller sections. It has the capacity of being calibrated to more than one stride length. It is a multifaceted, multitask, multi-capability instrument. It seemed to me that one would need a PHD in physics to understand the detailed instructions.

Nonetheless, after reading and rereading the instructions, I proceeded to calibrate my new pedometer. After several trial and error attempts (with much emphasis on error), I thought I had my half mile calibration distance recorded. I was wrong.

Lisa and I went on a hike with several friends. These experienced hikers estimated the hike to be approximately six miles. My pedometer recorded 1.8 miles. Obviously the pedometer wasn't calibrated correctly. "Operator error," the group was told by my lovely wife.

So I proceeded to re-calibrate. The next several attempts to re-calibrate by walking a pre-measured half mile resulted in that half mile being measured at 55.5 miles, 15.5 miles, 12.7 miles, and 99.3 miles. Needless to say, I have yet to figure out how to make this amazing gizmo work.

But, here's the real problem. While others on our hike were focused on the beauty of the mountains, the lake, the vegetation, the wildlife... I was focused on my stupid pedometer! I missed all the beauty I was in the midst of.

Sometimes the simplest things in life can cause the biggest frustrations. Like trying to hook up a new DVD player or trying to figure out how to work a digital camera or trying to get your teenager to clean their room or trying to pay your taxes or trying to decide which town council candidate to vote for or trying to pick something for dinner that every member of the family likes.

Sometimes the little things can cause us to take our eyes off the big things. I finally left the pedometer at home and just enjoyed the hike. Don't let the little frustrations in life take your eyes off the big blessings in life.

The Apostle Paul said, "So we fix our eyes not on what is seen, but on what is unseen. For what is seen is temporary, but what is unseen is eternal." 2 Corinthians 4:18.

It's a matter of focus. Let's keep our eyes on the big picture!

Riding A Mechanical Bull

A few years ago my family and I were in Puerto Vallarta, Mexico enjoying a great family vacation. We swam with dolphins, rode wave runners in the ocean, went kayaking, sailed on a Pirate ship, played at the beach, and had an all-around great time.

On one of the evenings, our resort hosted a Country Western night. It began with a buffet dinner and later the entertainment included a lasso demonstration, an energetic dance team, and line dance instructions. But the thing I'll remember the most is the mechanical bull.

I'd never ridden a mechanical bull before. And I don't plan on riding one ever again! But, at the encouragement of my family I did indeed jump on one while there. I slipped the operator some pesos and told him to make me look good. He smiled and nodded.

I climbed aboard and gave him a nod. The machine started to move slowly up and down and right and left. The operator said I was to slap the bull if I wanted to go faster. Faster?! Why in the world would I want to go faster?! I was doing just fine at this beginning speed. I held on with my right hand and tried to keep my left hand in the air above my head as I had been instructed.

But during one buck and turn, I brought my left hand down trying to maintain my balance. The operator must have mistaken this for a slap. So the mechanical bovine started going faster, with me on it. But not for long! Before you could say, "Howdy, Buckaroo" I was airborne. One minute I was sitting on the bull, the next I was in midair wondering if my medical insurance could be used in Mexico. I crashed to the mats, fortunately landing on a well-padded area.... my backside. I got up and limped back to my family. I sported a large, colorful bruise for several days.

Life is like that. One day we seem to be riding along, everything going fine. Then, with no warning at all, we've lost our grip and we're airborne. It may be the results of a medical test. It may be a surprise from the boss at work. It may be a decision our spouse has made. It may be the health of one of our family members. Any number of things can knock us out of the saddle and cause us to come crashing back to earth, bruised and limping.

Then what do you do?

We read in the book of Philippians, "...Forgetting what is behind and straining toward what is ahead, I press on toward the goal to win the prize for which God has called me heavenward in Christ Jesus." Philippians 3:13-14.

As the Apostle Paul said, you "press on." Bruises fade. Aches and pains eventually go away. Injuries heal. Lessons are learned: Things you would do differently; things you would never do again. Before long you are on to new adventures and life is good. You press on.

Have YOU ever ridden a mechanical bull? I know a place in Puerto Vallarta...

The North Rim

We were headed to the north rim of the Grand Canyon. I've been to the south rim several times, but I'd never been to the north rim. I've heard that it was different from the south rim. It's a much longer drive to get there, higher in elevation, cooler, more trees...different. So, early one Thursday morning, since we were already in the northern part of the state, Lisa and I found ourselves on the way to the north rim.

Along the way we passed many unexpected, unique places. We saw the old Navajo Bridge near Lee's Ferry. The bridge spans a spectacular gorge of tremendous depth. We stopped and took some pictures of the "Balancing Boulders," massive rocks precariously perched on thin columns of sediment. We enjoyed the beauty of the Vermillion Cliffs with their multicolored surfaces. We observed how quickly the vegetation changed as we drove out of the long, flat plains to the foothills and finally into the mountainous terrain.

Our favorite part of the drive was the last 45 miles. The road from Jacob's Lake to the lodge at the north rim cuts through some of the most beautiful forested land you'll ever see. Along with a variety of different types of pine trees, there is an abundance of majestic Aspen trees dotting the landscape. Large meadows of flowing grasses accent the stately forest.

We finally did reach our destination. The north rim of the Grand Canyon was, well, grand!   It truly is incredible to stand on cliff's edge, gazing into one of the seven wonders of the world.

The unique sites we saw on the way to the north rim didn't begin to compare to the splendor of the Grand Canyon. Nonetheless, each site had its own special attraction. Each one was a blessing to behold, in and of itself.

Life is like that. Our ultimate destination is Heaven. Nothing on this earth begins to compare to the splendor of Heaven. And yet, God sprinkles this life with a myriad of blessings, each with its own unique beauty and attraction. The trick for us is to not miss the blessings along the way. The presence of a special friend, a unique and cherished experience, a beautiful harmonious sound, a heartfelt relationship, a tender embrace, a colorful sunrise, tears of joy, the gentle rhythm of waves crashing upon a beach, the birth of a child, spontaneous laughter, the soft fur of a new puppy, the mesmerizing effect of a campfire, sitting on a porch swing at sunset... Life's journey is punctuated with blessings.

Romans 1:20, "For since the creation of the world God's invisible qualities — his eternal power and divine nature — have been clearly seen, being understood from what has been made."

Isn't it grand!

Family Pictures

A few years ago, a youngster was in my office and made an observation. She said, "You sure have a lot of pictures of your family in here." She was right! She noticed there were several pictures of my family on my desk, on my bookcase, on my credenza and on the shelves. There were 21 different pictures of my wife Lisa and my daughters, Andrea and Michelle. I know, because after she left, I counted them.

There were school pictures, pictures of the girls in their dance outfits, one of Andrea in her soccer uniform, one of the girls with their cousin Dani, several of Lisa and I, one of the girls and I walking in the woods near Sedona, and a few family photos taken in Maui. There was even one of the girls with our dog, Boaz! Some were taken long ago, some were taken recently.

I've been blessed with a gorgeous wife and two beautiful daughters. The photos are proof of that. But the pictures tell only half the story. It's their inner beauty that is really dazzling! To know their heart, to know their soul, to know their love of the Lord is to see their true beauty.

Did you know that God has your image etched in His mind? He sees you constantly.

Psalm 139:1-5
1   O LORD, you have searched me and you know me.
2   You know when I sit and when I rise; you perceive my thoughts from afar.
3   You discern my going out and my lying down; you are familiar with all my ways.
4   Before a word is on my tongue you know it completely, O LORD.
5   You hem me in--behind and before; you have laid your hand upon me.

God knows you intimately. In fact, he knows more about you than you do!

Matthews 10:30, "And even the very hairs of your head are all numbered."

God has your picture in His mind. Your image is constantly before Him. He knows when you are happy and when you are sad. He knows when you do good deeds and when you sin. He knows when you are frustrated and when you are excited. He knows when you are anxious and when you are content.

You are God's child. As such, you are loved with the deepest, purest, warmest, most perfect love that has ever existed. God's love for you is picture perfect!

Now, picture yourself in God's embrace: Doesn't that feel good!

Fireworks

Ka-Boom! Another firework exploded in the sky. I lit the fuse, turned and ran. Ka-Boom! The sky was filled with a bright flash and a spray of shining sparkles. The bottle rockets had all been launched. The sparklers had been lit and enjoyed by all. The other fireworks had already provided us their loud, shining entertainment. We only had six of the big ones left. The two-inch diameter ball was lowered down into the launching tube, fuse extending out the top. I lit another fuse and ran. A blast sent the explosive into the air and then... Ka-Boom!

We were in Rocky Point, Mexico. Fireworks are legal there, if exploded prior to 10:00 P.M. So there we were, on the beach, launching fireworks. Watching others who were also launching fireworks. It was fun. I was a kid again! Sure, I pretended to be doing this for the kids. But in all honesty, I enjoyed it as much as they did. Perhaps more. But the best part wasn't the pyrotechnics.

The best part of the trip was the fact that we were spending time together as a family. Watching fireworks. Laying on the beach. Bargain shopping. Going out to dinner. Watching the sunset from the top of the hill at the Casa Del Capitan Restaurant. Visiting the orphanage. Even the drive down and back. Time together as a family was far more enjoyable than an airborne explosion.

Did you know that studies show the number one memory adults have of their childhood is family vacations and special events and activities the family does together? There is much, much more going on during family vacation time than merely getting away from work or getting out of town. Family relationships are being nurtured. Lifelong memories are being created.

Kids grow up quickly. The window of opportunity closes. Let me encourage you to take a family vacation on a regular basis. It doesn't have to be elaborate or expensive or far away. It doesn't have to be punctuated with aerial blasts. Oftentimes the special times are found in the peaceful, simple times. Time is the key. Take time to spend time together.

The writer of the Book of Proverbs said, "Train a child in the way he should go, and when he is old he will not turn from it." Proverbs 22:6.

"Training" takes time. Quality time. I am convinced that quality time can't always be scheduled or planned, it is more often the spontaneous outgrowth of a quantity of time.

Do yourself and the kids a favor. Do something together as a family. You'll get a bang out of it!

Engine Trouble

As I was driving home I noticed smoke coming out from under the hood of my car. "That can't be good," I thought to myself. I looked at the dashboard gauges and didn't see any red lights or indicators displaying any kind of problem. The engine was running fine and the gauges were all normal. As I pulled into the driveway I could smell the distinct odor of a car which had just boiled over. What I had first thought was smoke was actually steam which was now billowing from all sides of the hood and from the front grille.

I lifted the hood to see if one of the radiator hoses had sprung a leak. They looked okay. Maybe I cracked the block? Maybe a freeze plug had blown out? I had no idea. So, I went into the house and called my son-in-law, the mechanic. Later that day he stopped by and took a look. In less than a minute, Josh had diagnosed the problem: a cracked thermostat housing hose connector. Later he fixed my car and I was up and running once again. Sure is nice to have an auto expert in the family!

There are some things I know a lot about, some things I know a little about, and many things I know nothing about. I guess that's true of everyone. Likewise, there are a few things I am really good at, some things I am okay at, and many things I am not good at. I guess that's true of everyone, too.

It certainly is true of all the members of the church. Each and every church member has strengths and weaknesses, things they are good at and things they are not as good at. But no one can do everything. That is why it is so important for every church member to discover what they are good at, what they are gifted at, and then serve the Lord in that area.

Romans 12:4-6 says, "Just as each of us has one body with many members, and these members do not all have the same function, so in Christ we who are many form one body, and each member belongs to all the others. We have different gifts, according to the grace given us..."

    If we will all use our gifts to serve the Lord and to serve each other, the church keeps running along and functioning at its optimum performance. Praise God for the church and the faithful members who keep it going!

Different

The difference is very striking.

The dessert area south of Lake Powell is very desolate, very barren. In my mind it is a very ugly, Godforsaken wasteland. But then one gets onto Lake Powell or into Antelope Canyon. The beauty is remarkable!

One of the first impressions of Lake Powell is how massive it is in size. Lisa and I rented a power boat and set off for Rainbow Bridge. Approximately 70 miles up the lake we reached our destination. However, we had only covered about one third of the length of the lake! Along the way we admired the beautiful red, orange, and gray cliffs. It truly is a beautiful oasis in the midst of the dessert.

Antelope Canyon is another jewel hidden among the sands and sagebrush of a desolate land. The canyon is approached through a typical dessert wash. Once inside the canyon, one stands in awe of the incredible creative beauty of our Heavenly Father. The sandstone walls of the narrow canyon reflect the limited light from the small openings at the top of the canyon. As the sun proceeds across the sky, the colors of the canyon wall continually change. It is indeed an inspirational location.

Monument Valley, with it's statuesque buttes and mesas, is also a sight to behold. Standing sentinel like, they can be seen for miles around, rising above the monotonous plain below.

The difference is very striking.

Did you know that Christians are supposed to be different!? The Apostle Paul wrote, "Do not conform any longer to the pattern of this world, but be transformed by the renewing of your mind..." Romans 12:2.

The Apostle Peter wrote, "Dear friends, I urge you, as aliens and strangers in the world, to abstain from sinful desires, which war against your soul. Live such good lives among the pagans that, though they accuse you of doing wrong, they may see your good deeds and glorify God on the day he visits us." 1 Peter 2:11-12.

We are supposed to be different. Not self-righteous or holier than thou. But different nonetheless. We are not to be like the rest of the world. We are to see things from an eternal perspective. We are to have heavenly priorities. We are to adhere to God's rules, morals and values, not that of man. We are to be in the world, but not of the world. We are to love all with a Christlike compassion. We are to care for others as needs arise. We are to make a difference, for the good. The difference should be very striking

Others should know that you are a Christian, not only because you tell them, but because they see a difference in your life. Strikingly different!

Emerald Canyon

Pinpoint accuracy. That's what it takes to play golf at Emerald Canyon. Pinpoint accuracy.

A group of us took a golf trip to Parker, (yes, Parker!) Arizona. We arrived in Parker Sunday evening and were up bright and early Monday morning for our first round at Emerald Canyon.

It's a very challenging course. It is wrought with peril. Several of the fairways wind their way through narrow canyons. In these narrow canyons there isn't even a rough. You are either in the fairway or you are out of bounds. You are either in the fairway or you are on top of a mountain or at the bottom of a cliff. There is no margin for error. You either hit a perfect shot, or you end up losing a golf ball and taking a penalty stroke. Pinpoint accuracy.

There are also several water hazards. The lake on hole number 12 claimed three of my brand new golf balls. And don't even talk to me about the sand traps!

If the Monday morning round weren't challenging enough, the afternoon round got worse. The wind picked up. Storm clouds gathered. The temperature dropped. A storm front was moving through. We didn't get rained out, but we nearly got blown off the course. Try hitting with pinpoint accuracy with a forty mile an hour cross wind.

Needless to say, I did not play a perfect round of golf that day. The hazards got me, time and time again.

There are many hazards in life. They are called sin. Life's fairways wind their way through narrow canyons with sin lurking on all sides. A variety of temptations are wrought with peril. The storms of life threaten to blow us out of bounds. These hazards get us time and time again. We fail to live a perfect life. Romans 3:23 says, "For all have sinned, and fall short of the glory of God." We do not have pinpoint accuracy in life. We miss the mark of perfection.

What's a person to do? In golf you take your penalty stroke and move on. Big deal. It's just a silly, insignificant game. But life is for real. And so is the consequence of sin. The Bible says that the wages of sin is death. (Romans 6:23). It also warns that you can be sure your sin will find you out. (Numbers 32:23).

The good news is that Jesus has taken the punishment for our sin. In spite of our failures, in spite of our mistakes, in spite of our sins... we have salvation. Not because of how good we are, but because of how good He is. Ephesians 2:8, "For it is by grace you have been saved, through faith-and this not from yourselves, it is the gift of God."

Sunday mornings provide the opportunity for Christians to "tee it up with the Lord" in worship and praise. You certainly don't need to be perfect. But you do need to show up!

Leaky Pipes

They say the third time's a charm. They are wrong! For the third time the main water line under the foundation at our home had a leak. The first two times the plumber came to our house, jack-hammered a hole in the foundation and fixed the leak. After the third time the plumber suggested that we would be better off to re-pipe the entire house. So, in hopes of avoiding an ongoing bi-monthly invasion of the plumber, we replaced the entire system.

What a mess! They had to cut holes in the walls and ceiling to run the new pipes. Then they had to patch, tape, texture and paint all the walls. They also had to put the carpet and pad back down. We were very glad when it was all finished!

The bottom line is that a patch here and a patch there just couldn't fix the faulty system. The only way to make it work right was to replace it with a new system.

The same is true in our spiritual lives. Sin leaks into our lives here and there. We try our best to patch the leak only to discover a new leak soon appears. What to do? A new system is needed!

Jesus doesn't just patch up the old you. He creates a whole new you!

2 Corinthians 5:17, "Therefore, if anyone is in Christ, he is a new creation; the old has gone, the new has come!"

Romans 6:6, "For we know that our old self was crucified with him so that the body of sin might be done away with, that we should no longer be slaves to sin"

This new creation begins with a new birth. John 3:3, "In reply Jesus declared, 'I tell you the truth, no one can see the kingdom of God unless he is born again.'"

If you are a Christian, you are a new creation! The old sins of the past have been done away with! There's now no reason for sin to leak into your life.

Unfortunately, all too often we want to try that old system

again. With predictable results. A leaky pipe will always leak. A sinful person will always sin.

Ephesians 4:22-24, "You were taught, with regard to your former way of life, to put off your old self, which is being corrupted by its deceitful desires; to be made new in the attitude of your minds; and to put on the new self, created to be like God in true righteousness and holiness."

In Christ you are a new creation. You can live a better life. The choice is yours: The old faulty you, or the new and improved version. Which will it be?

Gettysburg

During a recent visit to Pennsylvania, we spent a day at Gettysburg. We took a Segway tour of the battlefields. It was very informative! We began the tour at seminary ridge and ended at cemetery ridge. We saw the wide-open field of Pickett's fateful charge. We passed by the Peach Orchard, Devil's Den, Big and Little Round Top, and Culp's Hill. We ate lunch at a little restaurant which had been a farmhouse during the Civil War. Bullet holes can still be seen on the sides of the building. We also visited the Gettysburg National Cemetery where President Abraham Lincoln delivered his brief, but historic, Gettysburg Address.

It was a solemn experience to tour the grounds where approximately 50,000 American troops were killed. Several canons still remain at the sight. Rifles can be seen at museums and shops in town. Photos, taken in July of 1863 of dead soldiers laying in the fields where they had fallen, are also available. These young men gave their lives in service to their country. During his speech at the dedication of the cemetery, November of 1863, President Lincoln stated, "We cannot dedicate - we cannot consecrate - we cannot hallow - this ground. The brave men, living and dead, who struggled here, have consecrated it. Far above our poor power to add or detract."

Sadly, great nations are established and defended because men and women are willing to put their lives on the line for their country. This got me to thinking, what are we willing to do for the cause of Christ? What sacrifices are we willing to make? What hardships are we willing to endure? What inconveniences are we willing to tolerate?

The Apostle John stated, "This is how we know what love is: Jesus Christ laid down his life for us. And we ought to lay down our lives for our brothers." 1 John 3:16.

Jesus did not shy away from setting a high standard of expectation from His followers. He said, "If anyone would come after me, he must deny himself and take up his cross and follow me." Matthew 16:24.

Lay down our lives. Deny yourself. Sacrifice. Serve. These are not easy things to do. But those who change history, change destinies, change lives, do these very things. And when many like-minded people band together and do these things, incredible things happen.

So, let me ask, what are you willing to do for the cause of Christ?

Storms

I have always enjoyed the monsoon season in Arizona. Our area of Arizona gets half of our annual rainfall from these storms. As the monsoons roll in, you can see the huge, billowing thunder head clouds. From a distance the lightening illuminates the massive clouds. As the storm gets closer you begin to see individual lightning bolts in addition to the sudden flashes which brighten a large section of the sky. When the storm finally hits, you see and hear incredible strikes of lightening. The loud crackle and startling, sudden bang testify to the nearness of the strike. Lightning storms are an awesome display of the power of God.

For many, many years I have enjoyed these late summer dynamic storms. I usually sit on my patio, watching the lightning, wind, and rain. I love rain. Perhaps if I had grown up in a different part of the country I would feel differently. But I've spent most of my life in the desert where rain storms are infrequent. I'm sure that is why I'm fascinated by storms.

When I see lightning storms, I think about the return of Jesus Christ. His return will be the ultimate sensational event. While talking about his return, Jesus said in Matthew 24:27, "For as lightning that comes from the east is visible even in the west, so will be the coming of the Son of Man."

The Apostle Peter gave us a glimpse of that event when he wrote, "But the day of the Lord will come like a thief. The heavens will disappear with a roar; the elements will be destroyed by fire, and the earth and everything in it will be laid bare...That day will bring about the destruction of the heavens by fire, and the elements will melt in the heat. But in keeping with his promise, we are looking forward to a new heaven and a new earth, the home of righteousness." 2 Peter 3:10, 12-13.

WOW! That's going to be some show. Absolutely incredible!

Jesus encouraged His followers to be ready for His return. He said, "So you must be ready, because the Son of Man will come at an hour when you do not expect him." Matthew 24:44.

How does one prepare for the spectacular return of Jesus Christ? Jesus said, "For my Father's will is that everyone who looks to the Son and believes in Him shall have eternal life, and I will raise him up at the last day." John 6:40.

Half you placed your faith in Jesus as Lord and Savior? Are ready for that incredible day?

The Coffin

We sat and watched quietly as the coffin was unloaded from the airplane. Lisa and I were returning from a trip to Chicago and had just landed. They announced that our airplane was bringing home the remains of a gentleman who was in the U.S. military and had died while serving in Bosnia. His family was on the flight with us, his coffin in the lower compartment of the airplane. All passengers remained seated while the family left the plane and assembled on the tarmac. We watched out the window as a military Honor Guard was assembled. While that was happening, all the passengers left the plane. Lisa and I stopped at the gate and watched through the windows as the coffin was unloaded from the plane and loaded into a hearse. Meanwhile, bagpipes played, military personnel saluted, and local police and fire department personnel stood at attention.

But something else was also happening. Airplanes continued to land and take off. Other planes continued to taxi to and from the runway. People all around us continued to hurry to and from their gates, some stopping to grab a snack or visit one of the gift shops. A football game played on the TV in the waiting area of our gate. All around us, life just kept on going. The harsh reality is that we will all die. When that happens, life will continue on for everyone else, until their day arrives. The Bible states very matter-of-factly: "Just as man is destined to die once, and after that to face judgment." Hebrews 9:27.

Lessons learned? Several.

Make the most of each day. The days pass quickly and will come to an end before we are ready. Remember that the world doesn't revolve around you. For everyone else, life goes on.

Also, make sure you are ready for that day. By that I mean two things. First, don't leave your family guessing as to what you want done with your remains, what you want done at your funeral, what you want done with your estate, etc. Love them enough to take care of as much of these issues as you can before your fateful day.

Second, and most importantly, be prepared for what comes next. This life is very temporary. Eternal life follows. Don't be so consumed with this temporary life that you haven't taken care of your eternal destiny.

The Apostle John addressed this most critical issue when he wrote, "And this is the testimony: God has given us eternal life, and this life is in his Son. He who has the Son has life; he who does not have the Son of God does not have life." 1 John 5:11-12.

The Son of God, Jesus Christ, is the key to life beyond the coffin.

Have you received Jesus Christ as your Lord and Savior?

Made in the USA
Las Vegas, NV
07 May 2022

48563638R00062